KARMA/ NIRVANA

KARMA/NIRVANA

PAUL CARUS

ILLUSTRATIONS BY KWASONG SUZUKI

THE OPEN COURT PUBLISHING COMPANY
LA SALLE, ILLINOIS
1973

PAUL CARUS
(1852 - 1919)

He was editor of the Open Court Publishing Company
from 1887 to his death in 1919. As editor of two journals,
The Open Court and *The Monist,* and with the publication
of hundreds of books, many written by himself, he was a
pioneer in introducing the Orient to the West.

CONTENTS

Preface, ix

Publisher's Note, xi

Karma, 1

Nirvana, 47

PREFACE

This tale has greatly pleased me both by its art-
lessness and its profundity. The truth, much slurred
in these days, that evil can be avoided and good
achieved by personal effort only and that there exists
no other means of attaining this end, has here been
shown forth with striking clearness. The explanation is felicitous in that it proves that individual
happiness is never genuine save when it is bound
up with the happiness of all our fellows. From the
very moment when the brigand on escaping from
Hell thought only of his own happiness, his happiness ceased and he fell back again into his former
doom.

This Buddhistic tale seems to shed light on a
new side of the two fundamental truths revealed by
Christianity: that life exists only in the renunciation
of one's personality—"he that loseth his life shall
find it" (Matt. x. 39), and that the good of men is
only in their union with God, and through God with
one another—"As thou art in me and I in thee, that
they also may be one in us" (John xvii. 21).

I have read this tale to children and they liked it.
And amongst grown-up people its reading always

gave rise to conversation about the gravest problems of life. And to my mind this is the very best recommendation. . . .

It was only through a letter [from Paul Carus] that I learned *Karma* had been circulated under my name, and I deeply regret not only that such a falsehood was allowed to pass unchallenged, but also the fact that it really was a falsehood, for I should be very happy were I the author of this tale. It is one of the best products of national wisdom and ought to be bequeathed to all mankind, like the Odyssey, the History of Joseph, and Shakyamuni.

Count Leo Tolstoy

PUBLISHER'S NOTE

Soon after the appearance of *Karma* in the journal, *The Open Court,* requests for translations arrived from all over the world. These were granted, with the result that by the end of the nineteenth century, *Karma* had been published in three German renderings, two French, one Japanese, one Urdu, one Russian, Hungarian, Icelandic, and several Asian versions.

Karma appeared first in book form in Japan, where Open Court Publishing Company brought out three successive editions on crepe paper, illustrated in colors by Kwasong Suzuki. In the present editions, these illustrations, retouched by Eduard Biedermann, have been reproduced.

In this 1973 edition, *Karma* is being combined for the first time with another delightful Buddhist story, *Nirvana,* which was also written by Paul Carus, the editor and founder of Open Court Publishing Company.

KARMA

A STORY OF BUDDHIST ETHICS

DÊVALA'S RICE-CART

LONG, long ago in the days of early Buddhism, India was in a most prosperous condition. The Aryan inhabitants of the country were highly civilised, and the great cities were centres of industry, commerce, and learning.

It was in those olden times that Pandu, a wealthy jeweller of the Brahman caste, travelled in a carriage to Bârânasî, which is now called Benares. He was bent on some lucrative banking business, and a slave who attended to the horses accompanied him.

The jeweller was apparently in a hurry to reach his destination, and as the day was exceedingly pleasant, since a heavy thunderstorm had cooled the atmosphere, the horses sped along rapidly.

While proceeding on their journey the travellers overtook a samana, as the Buddhist

monks were called, and the jeweller observing
the venerable appearance of the holy man,
thought to himself: "This samana looks
noble and saintly. Companionship with good
men brings luck; should he also be going to
Bârânasî, I will invite him to ride with me in
my carriage."

Having saluted the samana the jeweller explained whither he was driving and at what
inn he intended to stay in Bârânasî. Learning that the samana, whose name was Nârada,
also was travelling to Bârânasî, he asked him
to accept a seat in his carriage. "I am
obliged to you for your kindness," said the
samana to the Brahman, "for I am quite
worn out by the long journey. As I have no
possessions in this world, I cannot repay you
in money; but it may happen that I can reward you with some spiritual treasure out of
the wealth of the information I have received
while following Shâkyamuni, the Blessed
One, the Great Buddha, the Teacher of gods
and men."

They travelled together in the carriage and
Pandu listened with pleasure to the instruc-

tive discourse of Nârada. After about an
hour's journey, they arrived at a place where
the road had been rendered almost impassable

by a washout caused by the recent rain, and a
farmer's cart heavily laden with rice prevented further progress.   The loss of a linch-

pin had caused one of the wheels to come off, and Dêvala, the owner of the cart, was busily engaged in repairing the damage. He, too, was on his way to Bârânasî to sell his rice, and was anxious to reach the city before the dawn of the next morning. If he was delayed a day or two longer, the rice merchants might have left town or bought all the stock they needed.

When the jeweller saw that he could not proceed on his way unless the farmer's cart was removed, he began to grow angry and ordered Mahâduta, his slave, to push the cart aside, so that his carriage could pass by. The farmer remonstrated because, being so near the slope of the road, it would jeopardise his cargo; but the Brahman would not listen to the farmer and bade his servant overturn the rice-cart and push it aside. Mahâduta, an unusually strong man, who seemed to take delight in the injury of others, obeyed before the samana could interfere. The rice was thrown on the wayside, and the farmer's plight was worse than before.

The poor farmer began to scold, but when

the big, burly Mahâduta raised his fist threat-
eningly, he ceased his remonstrances and
only growled his curses in a low undertone.

When Pandu was about to continue his
journey the samana jumped out of the carriage
and said: "Excuse me, sir, for leaving you
here. I am under obligations for your kindness in giving me an hour's ride in your carriage. I was tired when you picked me up on
the road, but now, thanks to your courtesy, I
am rested, and recognising in this farmer an
incarnation of one of your ancestors, I cannot
repay your kindness better than by assisting
him in his troubles."

The Brahman jeweller looked at the samana
in amazement: "That farmer, you say, is an
incarnation of one of my ancestors? That is
impossible!"

"I know," replied the samana, "that you
are not aware of the numerous important relations which tie your fate to that of the
farmer; but sometimes the smartest men are
spiritually blind. So I regret that you harm
your own interests, and I shall try to protect

you against the wounds which you are about
to inflict upon yourself.''

The wealthy merchant was not accustomed
to being reprimanded, and feeling that the
words of the samana, although uttered with
great kindness, contained a stinging re-
proach, bade his servant drive on without
further delay.

THE JEWELLER'S PURSE

THE samana saluted Dêvala, the farmer, and began to help him repair his cart and load up the rice, part of which had been thrown out. The work proceeded quickly and Dêvala thought: "This samana must be a holy man; invisible devas seem to assist him. I will ask him how I deserved ill treatment at the hands of the proud Brahman." And he said: "Venerable sir, can you tell me why I suffer an injustice from a man to whom I have never done any harm?"

And the samana said: "My dear friend, you do not suffer an injustice, but only receive in your present state of existence the same treatment which you visited upon the jeweller in a former life. You reap what you have sown, and your fate is the product of your deeds. Your very existence, such as it is now, is but the Karma of your past lives.''

"What is my Karma?" asked the farmer.

"A man's Karma," replied the samana, "consists of all the deeds both good and evil

that he has done in his present and in any prior existence. Your life is a system of many activities which have originated in the natural process of evolution, and have been transferred from generation to generation. The entire being of every one of us is an accumulation of inherited functions which are modified by new experiences and deeds. Thus we are what we have done. Our 'Karma' constitutes our nature. We are our own creators."

"That may be as you say," rejoined Dê-vala, "but what have I to do with that over-bearing Brahman?"

The samana replied: "You are in character quite similar to the Brahman, and the Karma that has shaped your destiny differs but little from his. If I am not mistaken in reading your thoughts, I should say that you would, even to-day, have done the same unto the jeweller if he had been in your place, and if you had such a strong slave at your command as he has, able to deal with you at his pleasure."

The farmer confessed, that if he had had the power, he would have felt little compunction in treating another man, who had happened to impede his way, as he had been treated by the Brahman, but thinking of the

retribution attendant upon unkind deeds, he
resolved to be in the future more considerate
with his fellow-beings.

The rice was loaded and together they pur-
sued their journey to Bârânasî, when sud-

denly the horse jumped aside. "A snake, a
snake!" shouted the farmer; but the samana
looked closely at the object at which the horse
shuddered, jumped out of the cart, and saw
that it was a purse full of gold, and the idea

struck him: "This money can belong to no one but the wealthy jeweller."

Nârada took the purse and found that it contained a goodly sum of gold pieces. Then he said to the farmer: "Now is the time for you to teach the proud jeweller a lesson, and it will redound to your well-being both in this and in future lives. No revenge is sweeter than the requital of hatred with deeds of good will. I will give you this purse, and when you come to Bârânasî drive up to the inn which I shall point out to you; ask for Pandu, the Brahman, and deliver to him his gold. He will excuse himself for the rudeness with which he treated you, but tell him that you have forgiven him and wish him success in all his undertakings. For, let me tell you, the more successful he is, the better you will prosper; your fate depends in many respects upon his fate. Should the jeweller demand any explanation, send him to the vihâra where he will find me ready to assist him with advice in case he may feel the need of it."

BUSINESS IN BENARES

To corner the market of the necessities of life is not a modern invention. The Old Testament contains the story of Joseph, the poor Hebrew youth who became minister of state, and succeeded with unscrupulous but clever business tricks in cornering the wheat market, so as to force the starved people to sell all their property, their privileges, and even their lives, to Pharaoh. And we read in the Jâtaka Tales that one of the royal treasurers of Kâsî, which is the old name of Bârânasî, made his first great success in life by cornering the grass market of the metropolis on the day of the arrival of a horse dealer with five hundred horses.

When Pandu the jeweller arrived at Bârânasî it so happened that a bold speculator had brought about a corner in rice, and Mallika, a rich banker and a business friend of Pandu,

was in great distress.   On meeting the jeweller he said : " I am a ruined man and can do
no business with you unless I can buy a cart
of the best rice for the king's table.   I have a
rival banker in Bârânasî who, learning that I
had made a contract with the royal treasurer
to deliver the rice to-morrow morning, and
being desirous to bring about my destruction,
has bought up all the rice in Bârânasî.   The
royal treasurer must have received a bribe,
for he will not release me from my contract,
and to-morrow I shall be a ruined man unless
Krishna will send an angel from heaven to
help me."

While Mallika was still lamenting the poverty to which his rival would reduce him,
Pandu missed his purse.   Searching his carriage without being able to find it, he sus-
pected his slave Mahâduta; and calling the
police, accused him of theft, and had him
bound and cruelly tortured to extort a confession.

The slave in his agonies cried : " I am innocent, let me go, for I cannot stand this
pain; I am quite innocent, at least of this

crime, and suffer now for other sins. Oh,
that I could beg the farmer's pardon whom,
for the sake of my master, I wronged without
any cause! This torture, I believe, is a punishment for my rudeness."

While the officer was still applying the lash
to the back of the slave, the farmer arrived at
the inn and, to the great astonishment of all
concerned, delivered the purse. The slave

was at once released from the hands of his torturer. But being dissatisfied with his master, he secretly left and joined a band of robbers in the mountains, who made him their chief on account of his great strength and courage.

When Mallika heard that the farmer had the best rice to sell, fit for delivery to the royal table, he at once bought the whole cartload for treble the price that the farmer had ever received. Pandu, however, glad at heart to have his money restored, rewarded the honest finder, and hastened at once to the vihâra to receive further explanation from Nârada, the samana.

Nârada said: "I might give you an explanation, but knowing that you are unable to understand a spiritual truth, I prefer to remain silent. Yet I shall give you some advice: Treat every man whom you meet as your own self; serve him as you would demand to be served yourself; for our Karma travels; it walks apace though, and the journey is often long. But be it good or evil, finally it will come home to us. Therefore it is said:

> 'Slowly but surely deeds
> Home to the doer creep.
> Of kindness sow thy seeds,
> And bliss as harvest reap.'"

"Give me, O samana, the explanation," said the jeweller, "and I shall thereby be better able to follow your advice."

The samana said: "Listen then, I will give you the key to the mystery. If you do not understand it, have faith in what I say. Self is an illusion, and he whose mind is bent upon following self, follows a will-o'-the-wisp which leads him into the quagmire of sin. The illusion of self is like dust in your eye that blinds your sight and prevents you from recognising the close relations that obtain between yourself and your fellows, which are even closer than the relations that obtain among the various organs of your body. You must learn to trace the identity of your self in the souls of other beings. Ignorance is the source of sin. There are few who know the truth. Let this motto be your talisman:

'Who injureth others
 Himself hurteth sore ;
 Who others assisteth
 Himself helpeth more.
 Let th' illusion of self
 From your mind disappear,
 And you'll find the way sure ;
 The path will be clear.'

"To him whose vision is dimmed by the dust of the world, the spiritual life appears to be cut up into innumerable selves. Thus he will be puzzled in many ways concerning the nature of rebirth, and will be incapable of understanding the import of an all-comprehensive loving-kindness toward all living beings."

The jeweller replied : "Your words, O venerable sir, have a deep significance and I shall bear them in mind. I extended a small kindness which caused me no expense whatever, to a poor samana on my way to Bârânasî, and lo! how propitious has been the result! I am deeply in your debt, for without you I should not only have lost my purse, but would have been prevented from doing business in

Bârânasî which greatly increases my wealth, while if it had been left undone it might have reduced me to a state of wretched poverty. In addition, your thoughtfulness and the arrival of the farmer's rice-cart preserved the prosperity of my friend Mallika, the banker. If all men saw the truth of your maxims, how much better the world would be! Evils would be lessened, and public welfare enhanced."

The samana replied: "Among all the religions there is none like that of the Buddha. It is glorious in the beginning, glorious in the middle, and glorious in the end. It is glorious in the letter and glorious in the spirit. It is the religion of loving-kindness that rids man of the narrowness of egotism and elevates him above his petty self to the bliss of enlightenment which manifests itself in righteousness."

Pandu nodded assent and said: "As I am anxious to let the truth of the Buddha be understood, I shall found a vihâra at my native place, Kaushambî, and invite you to visit me, so that I may dedicate the place to the brotherhood of Buddha's disciples."

AMONG THE ROBBERS

YEARS passed on and Pandu's vihâra at Kaushambî became a place in which wise samanas used to stay and it was renowned as a centre of enlightenment for the people of the town.

At that time the king of a neighboring country had heard of the beauty of Pandu's jewelry, and he sent his treasurer to order a royal diadem to be wrought in pure gold and set with the most precious stones of India. Pandu gladly accepted the order and executed a crown of the most exquisite design. When he had finished the work, he started for the residence of the king, and as he expected to transact other profitable business, took with him a great store of gold pieces.

The caravan carrying his goods was protected by a strong escort of armed men, but when they reached the mountains they were

attacked by a band of robbers led by Mahâduta, who beat them and took away all the
jewelry and the gold, and Pandu escaped with

great difficulty. This calamity was a blow to
Pandu's prosperity, and as he had suffered
some other severe losses his wealth was
greatly reduced.

Pandu was much distressed, but he bore his
misfortunes without complaint, thinking to
himself: "I have deserved these losses for
the sins committed during my past existence.

In my younger years I was very hard on
other people; because I now reap the harvest
of my evil deeds I have no reason for complaint."

As he had grown in kindness toward all beings, his misfortunes only served to purify
his heart; and his chief regret, when thinking of his reduced means, was that he had be-

come unable to do good and to help his friends
in the vihâra to spread the truths of religion.

Again years passed on and it happened that

Panthaka, a young samana and disciple of Nârada, was travelling through the mountains of Kaushambî, and he fell among the robbers in the mountains. As he had nothing in his possession, the robber-chief beat him severely and let him go.

On the next morning Panthaka, while pursuing his way through the woods, heard a noise as of men quarelling and fighting, and going to the place he saw a number of robbers, all of them in a great rage, and in their midst stood Mahâduta, their chief; and Mahâduta was desperately defending himself against them, like a lion surrounded by hounds, and he slew several of his aggressors with formidable blows, but there were too many for him; at last he succumbed and fell to the ground as if dead, covered with wounds.

As soon as the robbers had left the place, the young samana approached to see whether he could be of any assistance to the wounded men. He found that all the robbers were dead, and there was but little life left in the chief.

At once Panthaka went down to the little

brooklet which was murmuring near by, fetched fresh water in his bowl and brought it to the dying man. Mahâduta opened his eyes and gnashing his teeth, said: "Where are those ungrateful dogs whom I have led to victory and success? Without me as their chief they will soon perish like jackals hunted down by skilful hunters."

"Do not think of your comrades, the companions of your sinful life," said Panthaka, "but think of your own fate, and accept in the last moment the chance of salvation that is offered you. Here is water to drink, and let me dress your wounds; perhaps I may save your life."

"Alas! alas!" replied Mahâduta, "are you not the man whom I beat but yesterday? And now you come to my assistance, to assuage my pain! You bring me fresh water to quench my thirst, and try to save my life! It is useless, honorable sir, I am a doomed man. The churls have wounded me unto death — the ungrateful cowards! They have dealt me the blow which I taught them."

"You reap what you have sown," continued

the samana; "had you taught your comrades
acts of kindness, you would have received
from them acts of kindness; but having
taught them the lesson of slaughter, it is but
your own deed that you are slain by their
hands."

"True, very true," said the robber chief,
"my fate is well deserved; but how sad is
my lot, that I must reap the full harvest of
all my evil deeds in future existences! Advise
me, O holy sir, what I can do to lighten the
sins of my life which oppress me like a great
rock placed upon my breast, taking away the
breath from my lungs."

Said Panthaka: "Root out your sinful desires; destroy all evil passions, and fill your
heart with kindness toward all your fellow-
beings."

THE SPIDER-WEB

WHILE the charitable samana washed the wounds, the robber chief said: "I have done much evil and no good. How can I extricate myself from the net of sorrow which I have woven out of the evil desires of my own heart? My Karma will lead me to Hell and I shall never be able to walk in the path of salvation."

Said the samana: "Indeed your Karma will in its future incarnations reap the seeds of evil that you have sown. There is no escape from the consequences of our actions. But there is no cause for despair. The man who is converted and has rooted out the illusion of self, with all its lusts and sinful desires, will be a source of blessing to himself and others.

"As an illustration, I will tell you the story of the great robber Kandata, who died without repentance and was reborn as a demon in

Hell, where he suffered for his evil deeds the
most terrible agonies and pains. He had been

in Hell several kalpas and was unable to rise
out of his wretched condition, when Buddha
appeared upon earth and attained to the
blessed state of enlightenment. At that mem-
orable moment a ray of light fell down into
Hell quickening all the demons with life and
hope, and the robber Kandata cried aloud:
'O blessed Buddha, have mercy upon me! I
suffer greatly, and although I have done evil,
I am anxious to walk in the noble path of
righteousness. But I cannot extricate myself
from the net of sorrow. Help me, O Lord;
have mercy on me!'

"Now, it is the law of Karma that evil
deeds lead to destruction, for absolute evil is
so bad that it cannot exist. Absolute evil in-
volves impossibility of existence. But good
deeds lead to life. Thus there is a final end
to every deed that is done, but there is no end
to the development of good deeds. The least
act of goodness bears fruit containing new
seeds of goodness, and they continue to grow,
they nourish the poor suffering creatures in
their repeated wanderings in the eternal round

of Samsâra until they reach the final deliverance from all evil in Nirvâna.

"When Buddha, the Lord, heard the prayer of the demon suffering in Hell, he said : ' Kandata, did you ever perform an act of kindness? It will now return to you and help you to rise again. But you cannot be rescued unless the intense sufferings which you endure as consequences of your evil deeds have dispelled all conceit of selfhood and have purified your soul of vanity, lust, and envy.'

"Kandata remained silent, for he had been a cruel man, but the Tathâgata in his omniscience saw all the deeds done by the poor wretch, and he perceived that once in his life when walking through the woods he had seen a spider crawling on the ground, and he thought to himself, 'I will not step upon the spider, for he is a harmless creature and hurts nobody.'

"Buddha looked with compassion upon the tortures of Kandata, and sent down a spider on a cobweb and the spider said: 'Take hold of the web and climb up.'

"Having attached the web at the bottom of

Hell, the spider withdrew.   Kandata eagerly

seized the thin thread and made great efforts
to climb up.   And he succeeded.   The web

was so strong that it held, and he ascended
higher and higher.

"Suddenly he felt the thread trembling and
shaking, for behind him some of his fellow-
sufferers were beginning to climb up. Kandata became frightened. He saw the thinness
of the web, and observed that it was elastic,
for under the increased weight it stretched
out; yet it still seemed strong enough to carry
him. Kandata had heretofore only looked up;
he now looked down, and saw following close
upon his heels, also climbing up on the cobweb, a numberless mob of the denizens of
Hell. 'How can this thin thread bear the
weight of all?' he thought to himself, and
seized with fear he shouted loudly: 'Let go
the cobweb. It is mine!'

"At once the cobweb broke, and Kandata
fell back into Hell.

"The illusion of self was still upon Kandata. He did not know the miraculous power
of a sincere longing to rise upwards and enter
the noble path of righteousness. It is thin
like a cobweb, but it will carry millions of
people, and the more there are that climb it,

the easier will be the efforts of every one of them. But as soon as the idea arises in a man's heart: 'This is mine; let the bliss of righteousness be mine alone, and let no one else partake of it,' the thread breaks and he will fall back into his old condition of selfhood. For selfhood is damnation, and truth is bliss. What is Hell? It is nothing but egotism, and Nirvâna is a life of righteousness."

"Let me take hold of the spider-web," said the dying robber chief, when the samana had finished his story, "and I will pull myself up out of the depths of Hell."

THE CONVERSION OF THE ROBBER CHIEF

MAHÂDUTA lay quiet for a while to collect his thoughts, and then he addressed the samana not without effort:

"Listen, honorable sir, I will make a confession: I was the servant of Pandu, the jeweller of Kaushambî, but when he unjustly had me tortured I ran away and became a chief of robbers. Some time ago when I heard from my spies that Pandu was passing through the mountains, I succeeded in robbing him of a great part of his wealth. Will you now go to him and tell him that I have forgiven from the bottom of my heart the injury which he unjustly inflicted upon me, and ask him, too, to pardon me for having robbed him. While I stayed with him his heart was as hard as flint, and I learned to imitate the selfishness of his character. I have heard that he has be-

come benevolent and is now pointed out as an
example of goodness and justice. He has laid
up treasures of which no robber can ever de-

prive him, while I fear that my Karma will
continue to linger in the course of evil deeds ;
but I do not wish to remain in his debt so

long as it is still in my power to pay him. My
heart has undergone a complete change. My
evil passions are subdued, and the few mo-
ments of life left me shall be spent in the en-
deavor to continue after death in the good
Karma of righteous aspirations. Therefore,
inform Pandu that I have kept the gold crown
which he wrought for the king, and all his
treasures, and have hidden them in a cave
near by. There were only two of the robbers
under my command who knew of it, and both
are now dead. Let Pandu take a number of
armed men and come to the place and take
back the property of which I have deprived
him. One act of justice will atone for some
of my sins; it will help to cleanse my soul of
its impurities and give me a start in the right
direction on my search for salvation."

Then Mahâduta described the location of
the cave and fell back exhausted.

For a while he lay with closed eyes as
though sleeping. The pain of his wounds
had ceased, and he began to breathe quietly;
but his life was slowly ebbing away, and now
he seemed to awake as from a pleasant dream.

"Venerable sir," said he, "what a blessing for me that the Buddha came upon earth and taught you and caused our paths to meet and made you comfort me.   While I lay dozing I

beheld as in a vision the scene of the Tathâ-gata's final entering into Nirvâna.   In former years I saw a picture of it which made a deep impression on my mind, and the recollection of it is a solace to me in my dying hour."

"Indeed, it is a blessing," replied the samana, "that the Buddha appeared upon earth;
he dispelled the darkness begotten by ill will
and error, and attained supreme enlightenment. He lived among us as one of us, being subject to the ills of life, pain, disease,
and death, not unlike any mortal. Yet he
extinguished in himself all selfishness, all
lust, all greed for wealth and love of pleasure,
all ambition for fame or power, all hankering
after things of the world and clinging to anything transitory and illusive. He was bent
only on the one aim, to reach the immortal
and to actualise in his being that which cannot die. Through the good Karma of former
existences and his own life he reached at last
the blessed state of Nirvâna, and when the
end came he passed away in that final passing
away which leaves nothing behind but extin-
guishes all that is transitory and mortal. Oh,
that all men could give up clinging and
thereby rid themselves of passion, envy, and
hatred!"

Mahâduta imbibed the words of the samana
with the eagerness of a thirsty man who is

refreshed by a drink of water that is pure and cool and sweet. He wanted to speak, but he could scarcely rally strength enough to open his mouth and move his lips. He beckoned assent and showed his anxiety to embrace the doctrine of the Tathâgata.

Panthaka wetted the dying man's lips and soothed his pain, and when the robber chief, unable to speak, silently folded his hands, he spoke for him and gave utterance to such vows as the latter was ready to make. The samana's words were like music to the ears of Mahâduta. Filled with the joy that originates with good resolutions and entranced by the prospect of an advance in the search for a higher and better life, his eyes began to stare and all pain ceased.

So the robber chief died converted in the arms of the samana.

THE CONVERTED ROBBER'S TOMB

AS soon as Panthaka, the young samana, had reached Kaushambî, he went to the vihâra and inquired for Pandu the jew l-ler. Being directed to his residence he gave him a full account of his recent adventure in the forest. And Pandu set out with an escort of armed men and secured the treasures which the robber chief had concealed in the cave. Near by they found the remains of the robber chief and his slain comrades, and they gathered the bodies in a heap and burned them with all honors.

The ashes were collected in an urn and buried in a tumulus on which a stone was placed with an inscription written by Panthaka, which contained a brief report of Mahâduta's conversion.

Before Pandu's party returned home, Panthaka held a memorial service at the tumulus

in which he explained the significance of
Karma, discoursing on the words of Buddha:

नमो भगवत्या
आर्यप्रज्ञापारमिताये ॥

"By ourselves is evil done,
By ourselves we pain endure.
By ourselves we cease from wrong,
By ourselves become we pure.

No one saves us, but ourselves,
No one can and no one may :
We ourselves must walk the path,
Buddhas merely teach the way."

"Our Karma," the samana said, "is not the work of Ishvara, or Brahma, or Indra, or of any one of the gods. Our Karma is the product of our own actions. My action is the womb that bears me; it is the inheritance which devolves upon me; it is the curse of my misdeeds and the blessing of my righteousness. My action is the resource by which alone I can work out my salvation."

Then the samana paused and added:

"While every one is the maker of his own Karma, and we reap what we have sown, we are at the same time co-responsible for the evils of evil doers. Such is the interrelation of Karma that the errors of one person are mostly mere echoes of the errors of others. Neither the curse of our failings nor the bliss of our goodness is purely our own. Therefore when we judge the bad, the vicious, the criminal, let us not withhold from them our sympathy, for we are partners of their guilt."

Among the people of the surrounding villages the tumulus became known as ''The
Converted Robber's Tomb,'' and in later
years a little shrine was built on the spot
where wanderers used to rest and invoke the
Buddha for the conversion of robbers and
thieves.

THE BEQUEST OF A GOOD KARMA

PANDU carried all his treasures back to Kaushambî, and using with discretion the wealth thus unexpectedly regained, he became richer and more powerful than he had ever been before, and when he was dying at an advanced age he had all his sons, and daughters, and grandchildren gathered round him and said unto them:

"My dear children, do not blame others for your lack of success. Seek the cause of your ills in yourselves. Unless you are blinded by vanity you will discover your fault, and having discovered it you will see the way out of it. The remedy for your ills, too, lies in yourselves. Never let your mental eyes be covered by the dust of selfishness, and remember the words which have proved a talisman in my life:

'Who injureth others,
　Himself hurteth sore.
Who others assisteth,
　Himself helpeth more.
Let th' illusion of self
　From your mind disappear:
And you'll find the way sure;
　The path will be clear.'

"If you heed my words and obey these injunctions you will, when you come to die, continue to live in the Good Karma that you have stored up, and your souls will be immortalised according to your deeds."

NIRVANA

A STORY OF BUDDHIST PSYCHOLOGY

PREAMBLE

WHEN Buddha, the Blessed One, the Tathâgata, the great sage of the Sâkya tribe, was yet walking on earth, the news thereof spread over all the valley of the holy Ganga, and every man greeted his friend joyfully and said: "Hast thou heard the good tidings? The Enlightened One, the Perfect One, the holy teacher of gods and men, has appeared in the flesh and is bodily walking among us! I have seen him and have taken refuge in his doctrine; go thou also and see him in his glory. His countenance is beautiful like the rising sun; he is tall and strong like the young lion that has left his den; and when the Blessed One opens his mouth to preach, his words are like music, and all those who listen to his sermons believe in him. The kings of Magadha, of Kôsala, and of many other countries have heard his voice, have received him, and confess themselves his disciples. The Blessed Buddha has solved the riddle of the world and understands the problem of existence. He teaches that life is suffering, but he knows both the origin of suffering and the escape from it, and assures his disciples that Nirvâna can be obtained by walking in the noble path of righteousness."

SUDATTA, THE BRAHMAN YOUTH, AT THE PLOW

IN the fields of Kuduraghara, a small township of Avanti, there was a tall Brahman youth, by name Sudatta, plowing the grounds of Subhûti, who was called by the people Mahâ-Subhûti because he was wealthy, and whom the king had appointed chief of the village, to be a judge in all cases of law, both for the decision of litigations and the punishment of crimes.

Sudatta, while driving the draught-oxen, was merrily singing. He had good reason to be full of joy, for Mahâ-Subhûti, the chief, had chosen him for his son-in-law, and when, according to an old custom, the youth offered four clods to the maiden, one containing seeds, one ingredients from a cow-stable, one dust from an altar, and one earth taken from a cemetery, she had not touched the clod taken from the cemetery, which would have been an evil omen, but chose the clod containing dust from the altar, indicating thereby that her descendants would be distinguished priests and sacrificers. This was in Sudatta's opinion the noblest and most desirable fate. Rich harvests and prosperity in the raising of cattle were great blessings, but what are all worldly possessions in comparison to the bliss of religion! It was this idea that made Sudatta sing, and he was happy, even as Indra, the strong god, when intoxicated with the sweet juices of sôma.

Suddenly the plow struck the lair of a hare, and the hare jumped up to flee, but turned anxiously back to look after her brood. Sudatta raised the stick with which he goaded his oxen, chased the hare and sought to kill her, and would have accomplished his purpose had he not been interrupted by the voice of a man passing on the highroad, who called out: "Stay, friend! What wrong has that poor creature done?" Sudatta stopped in his pursuit and said: "The hare has done no wrong, except that she lives in the fields of my master."

The stranger was a man of serene appearance, and his shaven head indicated that he

was a samana, a monk, who had gone into homelessness for the sake of salvation. It was Anuruddha, a disciple of the Blessed One.

Seeing the plowman's noble frankness and the beauty of his appearance, he saluted him, and, as if trying to excuse the lad's conduct, the samana suggested: "You probably need the hare's flesh for meat."

"O, no!" replied the youth, "the flesh is not fit to eat in the breeding season. I chased the hare for sheer sport. Hares are quick, and there are but few boys who can outrun them."

"My dear friend," continued Anuruddha, "imagine yourself a parent whom some fierce giant deprived of his children and whom he hunted to death, as you intended to do unto this poor hare!"

"I would fight him," replied Sudatta eagerly, "I would fight him, though he might kill me."

"You are a brave boy," rejoined the samana, "but suppose the giant killed all your loved ones, your father and mother, your wife and children, and left you alive, mocking at your misery."

The youth stood abashed. He had never troubled his mind with such thoughts. He had never cared for creatures weaker than himself, and, for the sake of mere amusement, would not have hesitated to inflict pain on others. He was noble-minded and ambitious, eager to dare and to do, yet in one thing he was wanting.

Anuruddha thought to himself: "This youth is of a noble nature, but ill-advised. Should he remain uninstructed, his uncontrolled energy would do great harm. Would that he understood the religion of the Tathâgata, which is glorious in the letter and glorious in the spirit, true in its foundations, radiant as sunlight in its doctrines, and lofty in its practical applications. His manliness and courage, which would otherwise go to waste, might be turned to accomplish great things." And he addressed Sudatta saying: "Do you not know, friend, the words of the Tathâgata on behavior toward animals? The Blessed One said:

"'Suffuse the world with friendliness.
Let creatures all, both mild and stern,
See nothing that will bode them harm,
And they the ways of peace will learn.'

"This hare, like all other creatures in the

world, is possessed of sentiments such as you experience. She is, as much as you, subject to pain, old age, and death. You were not always strong and healthy. Years ago you were a tiny and helpless baby, and would not have lived but for the tender care of your loving mother and the protection of your dear father. You think of the present, forgetting your past and reckoning not on your future. As you no longer remember your suckling days, and know nothing of your state when you were safely sheltered in the womb of your mother, so you do not remember former existences in which your character developed in a gradual evolution to its present condition."

"Venerable man," said the youth, "you are a good teacher and I am willing to learn."

The samana continued: "Even the Tathâgata, our Lord, passed through all the stages of life in regular succession. By thoughts of truth, by self-control, and deeds of kindness he so fashioned his heart that he rose in the scale of beings until he became the Enlightened One, the perfect and Holy Buddha, and attained to Nirvâna. Æons ago he started on his earthly career in humble destitution and weakness. As a fish he swam in the ocean, as a bird he lived in the branches of trees and according to his deeds he passed from one form of existence to another. It is said, too, that he was a hare eking out a precarious existence in the fields. Did you never hear the tale?"

"No, never!" replied the youth, "tell me the story."

THE STORY OF THE HARE

ANURUDDHA began:

"So I have heard: Bôdhisatta once lived as a hare in the fields of a fertile country, and the hares waxed so numerous that food became scarce and they became a plague to the country.

"Then the thought occurred to Bôdhisatta while he was a hare: the times are hard and the people suffer for want of rice and wheat. They will rise in anger and slay all the hares that live in this country, and I, too, will have to die. Can I not do a noble deed lest in this present incarnation I live in vain? I am a weak creature and my life is useless unless I can contribute something, be it ever so little, toward the advance of enlightenment, for through enlightenment alone the bliss of deathless Nirvâna is attained. Let me seek Nirvâna. There is in this world such a thing as efficacy of virtue; there is efficacy of truth. Buddhahood is possible, and those who have attained Buddhahood by the wisdom of earnest thought and good deeds will show to others the path of salvation. The Buddhas' hearts are full of truth and compassion, of mercy and long suffering. Their hearts reach out in equal love to all beings that live. I will imitate them, and I will become more and more like them. The truth is one and there is but one eternal and true faith. It behooves me, therefore, in my meditation on the Buddhas, and relying on the faith that is in me, to perform an act of truth that will advance goodness and alleviate suffering.

"Having meditated on the path of salvation, Bodhisatta decided to warn his brother hares of the coming danger, to point out to them the instability of life, and to teach them the blessings of frugality and abstinence.

'And Bôdhisatta approached his brother hares and preached to them; but they would not listen to his words. They said: 'Go, thou, Brother Bôdhisatta, and perform a noble deed; go thou, and sacrifice thyself for the truth;

die that others may live, and take your chance
of being reborn in a higher and better incarnation. But do not inconvenience us with your
sermons. We love life and prefer the happiness which we enjoy, and which is real, to the
spread of truth, the bliss of which is a mere
assumption. There is plenty of maize and
wheat and rice and all kinds of sweet fruits in
the fields for us to eat. You need not worry
about us. Everybody must look out for himself.'

"Now, there was a Brahman who had retired into the woods for the sake of meditating
on the attainment of Nirvâna. And the Brahman suffered severely from hunger and cold.
He had lit a fire to keep himself warm after a
chilly shower; and stretching his hands over
the fire he bewailed his lot, saying: 'I shall
die before I have finished my meditation, for I
must starve for lack of food.'

"Bôdhisatta, seeing the worthy man in
need, said to himself: 'This Brahman shall
not die, for his wisdom may still be as a lamp
to many others who grope in darkness. I will
offer myself as food to him.' "With these

thoughts in his heart, Bôdhisatta jumped into

the fire offering himself as meat for him and
thus rescued the Brahman from starvation.

"Soon afterwards the people of the country, in fear of a famine, prepared a great hunt.
They set out all of them, on one and the same
day, and drove the hares into a narrow en-
closure, and in one day more than a hundred
thousand died under the clubs of the hunters."

WHAT IS NIRVÂNA?

WHEN Anuruddha had finished the story of the hare he said to Sudatta: "To live means to die. No creature that breathes the breath of life can escape death. All composite things will be dissolved again. Nothing can escape dissolution. But good deeds do not die. They abide forever. This is the gist of the Abhidharma. He who dares to surrender to death that which belongs to death, will live on and will finally attain to the blessed state of Nirvâna."

"What is Nirvâna?" asked the youth.

Anuruddha replied by quoting the words of the Great Master, saying:

"When the fire of lust is gone out then Nirvâna is gained.

"When the flames of hatred and illusion have become extinct then Nirvâna is gained.

"When the troubles of mind, arising from

pride, credulity, and all other sins, have ceased, then Nirvâna is gained."

The countenance of the youth betrayed his dissatisfaction with the new doctrines, and the Buddhist continued: "No one who still clings to the illusion of Self can understand, let alone taste, the sweetness of Nirvâna. All temporal existence is transient; all composite things have originated and will be dissolved again; and there is nothing abiding in bodily existence. Every concrete object has been moulded by its causes, and every individual organism has originated in the natural course of evolution, according to the conditions which determine its history. The constituents of being are in a constant flux, and there is nothing that could be regarded as a permanent Self, as an immortal being, as an entity of any kind that would remain identical with itself. Know, then, that which remains identical with itself, that which is eternal, that which is absolutely immutable and permanent, is not a concrete being, not a material body of any description, not a particular and individual existence; not a Self of any kind. And yet it exists! The

deathless, the immortal and immutable, is
an actuality; it is the most significant and important actuality in the world, but this actuality is spiritual, not substantial. And what is
it? The deathless, which in its omnipresence
is immutable and eternal, is the Bôdhi; it is
the harmony of all those verities that remain
the same forever and aye. The truths on which
the wise rely when they argue are not particular things, not single facts, not concrete
entities, not Selfs of any kind, neither gods
nor animate beings; they are nothing—if
nothing means the absence of any concrete
thingishness or special selfhood; and yet their
nothingness is not a non-existence. If the
deathless, the immortal, the immutable, did
not exist, there would be no escape from the
sufferings of the world. If the Bôdhi were an
illusion there would be no enlightenment;
Nirvâna could not be attained and no Buddha
could ever appear to point out the way of salvation. But the Buddha hath appeared; he
hath understood the utter groundlessness of the
belief in an immutable Self; he hath discovered
that all misery consists in the clinging to Self;

and he pointeth out the way of salvation,
through the attainment of the Bôdhi, leading
all those who honestly seek the light, on the
eightfold noble path of righteousness, to the
glorious and deathless Nirvâna.''

"Venerable man,'' said Sudatta, ''the noble
Sâkyamuni of whom you learned the doctrine that you proclaim seems to be a great
master; yet he will not be honored in Kuduraghara, for we are all good orthodox Brahmans, and there is not one follower of the Buddha among us   Nevertheless, I must not con-
ceal from you that there is one man in our
village who speaks highly of Sâkyamuni.   It
is Mahâ-Subhûti, a friend of king Bimbisâra,
the judge and chief of the township.   If you
enter the village go to him and he will receive
you. Not that he is a follower of the Buddha,
but a friend of his by personal attachment, for
he has met Gautama at the king's court and he
says : ' Should Brahma, the god, ever descend
upon earth he would appear like Gautama ; for
surely Brahma could not look more majestic
nor more divine than the noble Sâkyamuni.'
When you meet Subhûti, the chief, greet him

in my name, in the name of Sudatta, the son
of Rôja, and he will invite you to witness the
marriage of his daughter, which shall take
place to-morrow. Go then to the house of
Mahâ-Subhûti, and there I shall meet you,
for I am the man to whom his daughter is be-
trothed.''

BEGGING FOR ALMS

WHEN Anuruddha entered Kuduraghara, the Brahman village on the precipice near Kuduraghara, he hesitated a moment and thought to himself: "What shall I do? Shall I go to Mahâ-Subhûti, or shall I go from house to house according to the rules of the order of samanas?" And he decided: "The rule must be followed. I will not go to Mahâ-Subhûti, but will go from house to house."

With form erect and eyes cast down, holding his bowl in his left hand, the samana placed himself in front of the first house, patiently waiting for alms. As no one appeared at the door, the slender figure moved on. Many refused to give him anything, sending him away with angry words. Even those who offered him a small portion of rice called him a heretic; but as he was free from desire as to his personal concerns, he blessed the donors;

and, when he saw that he had enough to satisfy·
the needs of the body, he turned back to eat

his modest meal under the green trees of the
forest. While crossing the square of the village, there appeared in the door of the town

hall a dignified Brahman, who, after a searching glance at the stranger, stopped him and
asked: "Art thou a disciple of the Blessed
One, the Holy Buddha?"

"I am Anuruddha, a disciple of the Blessed
One," replied the samana.

"Well, well," said the Brahman, "I should
know you, for I have met the Blessed One at
Râjagaha, and he spoke with admiration of
Anuruddha as a master in metaphysics and a
philosopher who has grasped the doctrine of
the Tathâgata. If you are indeed Anuruddha, I welcome you to my house. Do me the
honor, O venerable samama, of staying with
me at my house; deign to take your meal at
my residence. And I shall be glad if you will
grace with your presence the marriage of my
daughter, which will take place to-morrow."

"Allow me, O chief of Kuduraghara," replied Anuruddha "to eat my meal in the
forest, and to-morrow I shall come and witness the marriage of your daughter."

"Be it so!" said Subhûti. "You will be
welcome whenever you come."

THE WEDDING

SUBHÛTI'S mansion was decorated with flags and garlands, and a bridal reception-hut was built of bamboo in the courtyard over the fireplace. The inhabitants of Kudura-ghara were waiting at the door to watch the procession.

Sudatta, the groom, appeared in festive attire with his friends and approached reverently the father of the bride. The venerable Brahman chief received the young man cordially and led him to the family altar in the presence of his wife, the bride's mother, and his only son Kacchâyana. There he offered to the groom the honey drink, and presented to his daughter the bridal gown with a costly head ornament and a necklace of jewels.

Addressing the groom he said: "It behooves a Brahman father to select as husband for his daughter, a Brahman maiden of pure

caste, a Brahman youth, the legitimate son of
Brahman parents, and to marry the couple according to the Brahma-rite. I have chosen
thee, O Sudatta, for thou art worthy of the
bride. Thou art of Brahman caste, thy bones,
thy knees, thy neck, thy shoulders are strong.
The hair of thy head is full, thy skin is white,
thy gait is erect, and thy voice is clear. Thou
art well versed in the Vêda and of good conduct. Thy parents are respected in the village, and I am confident that you will fulfil all
the duties of a good husband. My daughter

shall be thy lawful wife, loyal in adversity as
well as in good fortune, and may the children

that shall be born to thee, and thy children's
children, be worthy of their ancestors in the
line of either parent. The bride is ready

in her bridal garments. Receive her and perform the duties of life in unison.''

The sacrifices were properly performed according to the traditions of the country, and

while the highest priest of the village recited
the Mantra, the father of the bride poured out

the water libation. The groom clasped the
maiden's hand, and she stepped upon the
stone of firmness. Then the young couple

performed the ceremony of circumambulat-
ing the altar in seven steps, indicating that
they would henceforth be partners in life and
meet all changes of fate, whether good or evil,
in unison.

Thereupon the married couple, preceded
by the groomsman Kacchâyana, the bride's
brother, the bridesmaids, and all the guests,
started for the groom's house, the future home
of the bride. Fire from the altar on which
the burnt offerings had been consumed was
carried in an iron pan by a priest who followed
the bridal carriage.

While the bridal procession was passing
through the street, the people hailed the bride
and threw handfuls of rice over her with in-
vocations and blessings. At Sudatta's residence, the groom carried the bride over the
threshold. The new hearth fire was lit with
the flames of the bridal altar, and when the
prescribed sacrifice was made, the young couple
circumambulated the holy fire of Agni three
times. Then they sat down on the red cow-
hide spread out before them, and a little boy,
a relative of the family, was placed in the

bride's lap, while the brother of the groom's deceased father, a venerable old priest, prayed over her: "May Agni, who blazes forth with hallowed flame upon the hearth of the house, protect thee! May thy children prosper and see the fulness of their days! Be thou blessed, O worthy maiden, in thy bridal beauty as a mother of healthy children, and mayest thou behold the happy faces of vigorous sons!"

Then the groom gave a handful of roasted barley to the bride and said: "May Agni bestow blessings upon the union of our hands and hearts!"

A SERMON ON HAPPINESS

AFTER the completion of the wedding ceremonies, Subhûti invited his guests to partake of a meal, and seeing among the people Anuruddha, the philosopher, he called him to sit at his side. The guests were merry and enjoyed the feast, and when the evening grew cooler and the moon rose in mild radiance, the company sat down under the branches of a large banyan tree and began to speak of the blessings of the gods and the glory of their country. Then Subbûti, the judge, addressed Anuruddha and said:

"Venerable Anuruddha, I cherish a high regard for the Blessed One, the sage of the Sâkyas, whom the people call the Tathâgata, the Holy Buddha. But it seems to me that his doctrine will not suit our people. It is a philosophy for those who are oppressed by the evils of life; it affords a refuge to the weary, the sick, the sorrowing; but with the happy, the powerful, the healthy, it must be a failure. It may be a balm for those that are wounded in the battle, but it is distasteful and like unto poison to the victor."

Said Anuruddha: "The doctrine of the Blessed One is indeed for those who are oppressed by the evils of life. It affords a refuge to the weary, for it secures to them health and happiness. The happy, the powerful, the hale, need no comfort, no assistance, no medicine. But who are hale, happy, and healthy? Is there any one among you free from the liability to sorrow, disease, old age, and death? If so, he might truly be called a victor, and he would not be in need of salvation.

"Now, indeed, I see here much happiness around me. But is your happiness well grounded? Will your minds remain serene and calm in the time of affliction and in the hour of death? He only has attained genuine happiness who has entered the deathless Nirvâna, that state of heart which lifts above the petty temptations of the world and liberates from the illusion of Self. Happiness on account of

worldly prosperity is a dangerous condition;
for all things change, and he only is truly
happy who has surrendered his attachment to
things changeable. There is no genuine happiness except it be grounded upon religion,
the religion of the Tathâgata.

"The Tathâgata opens the eyes of those
who deem themselves happy that they may
see the dangers of life and its snares. When
the fish perceives the bait he believes he is
happy, but he feels his misery as soon as the
sharp hook pierces his jaws.

"He who is anxious about his personal
happiness must always be full of fear. He may
be indifferent to the misery of his fellow-beings, but he cannot be blind to the fact that
the same end awaits us all. Happy he who
resigns to death that which belongs to death.
He has conquered death; whatever be his fate,
he will be calm and self-possessed; he has
surrendered the illusion of Self and has entered the realm of the immortal. He has attained to Nirvâna."

Sudatta looked at the bride and said: "I
shall never embrace Gautama's doctrine, for it

would not behoove a groom to leave his bride
for the sake of the attainment of Nirvâna.''

Anuruddha overheard Sudatta's remark
and continued : ''My young friend fears that
the doctrine of the Tathâgata would tear him
away from the bride to whom to-day he has
pledged his troth. That is not the case. The
Blessed One left his wife and child and went
into homelessness because error prevails and
the world lies in darkness. Having reached
the deathless Nirvâna, he is now bent alone on
the one aim of pointing out the path to others,
and we, his disciples, who like him have left
the world, devote ourselves to a religious life,
not for our own sake, for we have released all
attachment to Self, but for the sake of the
salvation of the world. Our maxim is expressed in the one word *anattavâdo*, the non-
assertion of self.

''It is not the severing of the ties of life
that constitutes liberation, but the utter surrender of Self. The hermit who has cut himself off from the world but still cherishes in
his heart the least inkling of desire, lust-
ing for happiness in this life or in a life to

come, is not yet free, while a humble house-
holder, if he has surrendered all craving, may
attain that glorious condition of soul, the frui-
tion of which is Nirvâna.

"He who longs for a religious life should
leave worldly considerations behind, and apply
himself with all his energy to obtain enlightenment. But he who has duties to perform at home should not shirk his responsi-
bility. The Tathâgata says:

> "'Cherish father and mother,
> And wife and children: this
> And love of a peaceful calling,
> Truly, is greatest bliss.

> "'Practising lovingkindness,
> Befriending one's kindred: this
> And to lead a life that is blameless,
> Truly, is greatest bliss.

> "'Self-control and wisdom,
> The four noble truths,—all this,
> And attainment of Nirvâna,
> Truly, is greatest bliss.'"

THE CONTROVERSY

ANURUDDHA saw that Sudatta was filled
with indignation. So he ceased to speak
and looked expectantly at the young man.
Sudatta rose to his feet and said:

"Utter surrender of Self? Is that the liberation which Gautama preaches? My father called
him a heretic and an infidel, and truly he was
not mistaken, for Gautama's liberation is a destruction: it annihilates man's Self. Gautama
rejects the authority of the sacred Scriptures.
He does not believe in Ishvara, the Lord of
Creation, and he holds that there is no soul.
Yea, he is so irreligious that he condemns
sacrifices as impious, ridicules prayer as useless, and would fain destroy our sacred institution of castes on which the social order of our
civilisation rests. His religion is the negation
of all religion, it is not divine but purely hu-
man, for it rejects belief in the divinity of the

Vedas and claims that enlightenment is suffi-
cient to illumine the path of life."

Anuruddha listened to Sudatta's vehement
denunciations, and observing the heightened
color in his cheeks, thought to himself: "How
beautiful is this lad and how noble does he appear in his pious zeal for the religion of his
father!" Then he said: "The Tathâgata does
not oppose Brahmanism. He who has grasped
his doctrines will understand that he is a re-
former. He revealed to us a higher interpreta-
tion of religion."

Replied Sudatta: "A denial of the existence of the Self will destroy all religion."

Anuruddha asked: "What do you mean by
Self?"

Sudatta, who was well trained in the Ve-
dânta philosophy, said: "My Self is the immutable eternal Ego that directs my thoughts.
It is that which says 'I.'"

"What is the Ego or that which says 'I'?"
exclaimed Anuruddha: "There is unquestion-
ably something which says 'I' in me, and in
you, and in everybody present. But when
we say 'I,' it is a mode of speech, as much

as are all the other words and ideas that
people our minds. The word 'I,' it is true,

remains the same throughout life, but its
significance changes. It originates in the child

with the development of self-consciousness, and denotes first a boy, then a youth, after that a man, and at last a dotard. The word may remain the same, but the substance of its meaning changes. Accordingly, that something which says 'I,' is neither eternal, nor immutable, nor divine, nor what Yoga philosophers call 'the real Self.' It is a word which signifies the whole personality of the speaker with all his sensations, sentiments, thoughts, and purposes."

The Brahman replied: "Gautama is an infidel who denies the existence of the soul, and yet is so inconsistent as to talk about rebirth in future incarnations, and of immortality."

"Let us not haggle about words, friend Sudatta," said the samana, "but understand the doctrine aright. The Tathâgata looks upon that assumedly immutable ego-self of which you speak as an error, an illusion, a dream; and attachment to it will produce egotism which is a craving for happiness either here on earth or beyond in heaven. But while that illusory Self is an error of your philosophy, your personality is real. There is not a person who is in possession of character, thoughts, and deeds; but character, thoughts, and deeds themselves are the person. There is not an ego in you, O Sudatta, that thinks your thoughts and shapes your character, but your thoughts themselves are thinking, and your character itself is the nature of your very self. Your character, your thoughts, your volitions are you yourself. You have not ideas, but you are ideas."

"But who is the lord of these ideas of mine?" asked Sudatta. "Here your theory is wanting. Blessed is he who knows that the lord of his ideas is his ego, his Self."

Anuruddha continued: "The ego-idea is not a lord who owns your body and mind, directing the emotions and impulses of your character; but those of your emotions which are the strongest, they are the Lord, they govern you. If evil passions grow in your heart, you will be like a ship which is at the mercy of the winds and the currents of the sea; but if the aspiration for enlightenment takes possession of you, it will steer you to the haven of Nirvâna where all illusions cease and

the heart will be tranquil like a still, smooth
lake. Deeds are done; and the doing of deeds
passes away; but that which is accomplished
by deeds abides; just as a man who writes a
letter ceases writing, but the letter remains.
Considering the permanence that is in deeds,
what can be better than shaping our future
existence wisely? Lay up a treasure of charity,
purity, and sober thoughts. He who lives in
noble thoughts and good deeds will live forever, though the body may die. He will be
reborn in a higher existence and will at last
attain the bliss of Nirvâna. There is no trans-
migration of a self-substance, but there is a
re-incarnation of thought-forms which takes
place according to the deeds that are done."

"The Buddha teaches that good deeds
should be done vigorously, and only the bad
volitions which are done from vanity, or lust,
or sloth, or greed, should be eradicated."

Sudatta's belief in the doctrine of the Self
was not shaken. No, he felt more assured than
ever of its truth, for his whole religion hung on
it, and he exclaimed: "What are my deeds

without my Self? What is enjoyment if I am not the enjoyer?"

Anuruddha's pensive countenance grew more serious than ever: "Dismiss the craving for enjoyment and all thought of Self and live in your deeds for they are the reality of life. All creatures are such as they are through their deeds in former existences. The thought-forms are the realities of our spiritual life. They are transferred from one individual to another. Individuals die, but their thought-forms will be reincarnated according to their deeds. Deeds shape in the slow process of growth the thought-structures which build up our personality, and that which you call the person, the enjoyer, the Self, is the totality of your thought-forms, the living memory of past deeds. Deeds done in past existences are stamped upon each creature in the character of his present existence. Thus the past has borne the present, and the present is the womb of the future. This is the law of Karma, the law of deeds, the law of cause and effect."

"You take away the unity of the soul," replied Kacchâyana.

"Say rather," rejoined Anuruddha, "I insist upon the complexity and wealth of man's spiritual nature. So long as the illusion of self is upon you, you cannot reach Nirvâna."

The samana's words were weighty and serious. Nevertheless, his auditor remained unconvinced, and Kacchâyana murmured to himself: "Gautama's doctrine cannot be the truth. It would be a sad truth, indeed, if it were true after all. I shall hold fast to the dearest hope of the religion of my father."

The samana replied: "Choose not the dearest but the truest; for the truest is the best."

THE KATHA-UPANISHAD

SUDATTA was too happy to give himself trouble about the doctrines of a heretical teacher. He would have dismissed all thought of his controversy with Anuruddha, had he not been reminded of it from time to time by his father-in-law and by Kacchâyana, his brother-in-law, who continued to discuss the religious innovations of the Tathâgata. They granted that caste distinctions were hard on the lower castes, but declared that they could not be relaxed without injury to the community, and there was no question about its being a divine institution. Yet it was right to extend our sympathy to all sentient beings that suffer, and the lowest creatures should not be excepted. Certainly we must not by negligence of worship provoke the wrath of the gods; but were the gods truly in need of the bloody sacrifices offered at their altars?

Such were the questions that moved the
minds of Subhûti and Kacchâyana; and they

began to doubt while they investigated; yet
they remained good Brahmans.

One day Subhûti, the chief of Kuduraghara,

came to his son with a joyful countenance and said: "Kacchâyana, my boy, I trust that I have found the solution of the problem. It

came to me while I was preparing myself for a performance of the Nâchiketas fire-sacrifice, after the manner of the Katha school. While reading the Yajur-Veda, I understood the dif-

ficulties and all doubts were resolved. Take
leaves from the big palm-tree in our garden,
and bleach them, cut off their pointed ends
and prepare them for writing. I am eager to
give a definite shape to my thoughts before I
forget them.''

Said Kacchâyana with ardent expectation:
'' And what in brief is the solution you have
arrived at? ''

The Brahman chief replied: '' Listen, I will
tell you. Death is the great teacher of the
deepest problems of life. He who wants to
know the immortal must enter the house of
Death and learn from death the secret of life.
There is no child born in this world but is
destined to be an offering to Death. Yet Death
is not Brahma, he is not the ruler and lord;
he portends dissolution but cannot annihilate
the soul, and the man who fears him not is
granted three boons. Death allows those who
enter his house to return and be reborn; he
further concedes that the deeds of men shall
be imperishable; and lastly he reveals to the
courageous inquirer the mystery of life.''

Said Kacchâyana: '' Profound, O father, are

these thoughts; but the main thing is, What is the lesson Death teaches?''

Subhûti collected his thoughts, and after a pause said: ''The doctrine of the Blessed One has deeply affected my mind, but I am not as yet convinced that the fundamental notions of our sacred religion are baseless. Is the great fire sacrifice indeed an empty ceremony that bears no fruit? If it were, our sages would truly be, as says the Sakyamuni, blind leaders of the blind. Sacrifices are without fruit to him only who has not conquered the desires of his heart and has not severed the ties which bind him to that which is transient.''

After a brief pause Subhûti continued: ''And the idea of an immutable Self cannot be mere fiction. I understand now that the Self is the uncreated and the sole ruler within all things, yet it cannot be seen by the eye, reached by the speech or apprehended by the mind; the Self must be imagined by the heart. The Self is briefly expressed in the exclamation 'Om,' and is the absolute being which is neither born nor dies.''

''Your solution, then,'' continued Kacchâyana, "though a new Brahmanism is a justification of the old?"

"Indeed it is," enjoined Subhûti, "but my attitude is considerably modified by the suggestions of our friend Anuruddha. I grant that that which is good is one thing and that which is dear to our hearts is another thing; and it is well to cling to the good and abandon, for the sake of the better, that which is dear to our hearts. I cannot deny the truth which the Tathâgata impresses upon the minds of his followers, that all compounded things will be dissolved, but I feel in my inmost heart that there is something which death cannot destroy; and it is that which our sages call the Self. I am anxious to know what it is, for only he who knows it will find peace of soul. Let Anuruddha explain to me the problem of the Self, but he must not say that there is nothing that I can call my own, that life is empty, and that the eternal has no existence."

✻   ✻   ✻

During the rainy season Subhûti could be seen writing in the shelter of his veranda, and

when the sun broke through the clouds and
the blue sky reappeared in its former beauty
he had his treatise finished, which he called
the Katha-Upanishad.

THE IMMORTALITY OF DEEDS

IT was in these days of the return of good weather that the disciples of the Blessed Buddha were wont to start out on their pilgrimages through the country preaching the glorious doctrine of salvation, and Anuruddha passed again through the village of Avanti while Subhûti sat before his house in the shade of a sala tree reading and reconsidering what he had written. The two men exchanged greetings, and when Anuruddha saw the manuscript, they at once began to discuss the great problem of the Hereafter.

Subhûti read to Anuruddha the Katha-Upanishad, and the venerable monk was greatly pleased with its literary beauty and thoughtfulness, but he shook his head and said: "Truly there is the immortal, but the immortal is not a Self, the immortal is not a being, it is not an entity, nor is it the ego that

appears in our perception of consciousness.
All things, all beings, all entities, all shapes
of substances are compounds, and compounds
are subject to dissolution. The immortal is
not as you have it smaller than small and
greater than great; it is neither small nor
great; it is unsubstantial and without bodily
shape. The immortal consists in the eternal
verities by which existence is swayed; it is
the immutable law of life the cognition of
which constitutes enlightenment. The highest
verities are the four noble truths, of misery,
the origin of misery, the escape from misery,
and the eightfold path of righteousness, which
leads to the escape from misery."

Said Subhûti: " I grant that the eternal cannot be a material thing; the eternal cannot be
a compound; it must be immaterial; it is
spiritual. The self is not the body, not the
senses, not the mind, not the intellect; it is
that by which man perceives all objects in
sleep or in waking. The consciousness 'I am'
is the great omnipresent Self, which is bodi-
less within the body, as agni, the fire, lies
hidden in the two fire sticks."

Anuruddha paid close attention to Subhûti's
expositions, and replied in quick repartee:
"Agni, the fire, does not lie hidden in the two
fire sticks. The two fire
sticks are wood, nothing
but wood; and there is no
fire hidden in either stick.
The fire originates through
the friction produced by
your hands. In the same
way consciousness origi-
nates as a product of conditions and disappears when
the conditions cease. When
the wood is burnt, whither
does the fire go? And when
the conditions of consciousness cease, where does consciousness abide? "

"My friend," said
Subhûti, " we must
distinguish between the thing and its phenom-
enon; between Agni and the flame; between
consciousness and its manifestations; between
the person and the properties of a person, his

faculties or activities; between the wind and the commotion which the wind creates."

"Must we?" asked musingly the Brahman chief's guest. "It is true, we are in the habit of saying 'the wind blows,' as if there were the wind performing the action of blowing; but there are not two things: first the wind, and then the act of blowing; there is only one thing, which is the motion of the air, called wind, or, by a license of speech, we speak of the blowing of the wind. In the same way there is not a person that remembers deeds, but the memories of the deeds are themselves the person."

"When a man is dead," enjoined Subhûti, "some say he exists, and others he exists not. I understand that the Blessed One teaches that he no longer exists, which means, to put it squarely, that there is no hereafter."

"No, sir," Anuruddha answered almost sharply: "No, sir. Your dilemma rests upon a wrong premise. That Self of yours does not now exist, how then can it continue to exist after you have gone? That, however, which you are now, will persist after the termination

of your bodily existence. Truly you are right
when you compare man in your Katha-Upanishad to that ancient tree whose roots grow
upward and whose branches grow downward.
As the tree reappears with all the character-
istics of its kind, so man is reincarnated, and
his peculiar karma is reborn in new individuals. There is no Self in the fig-tree that mi-
grates from the parent stem to the new shoots,
but the type in all its individual features is
preserved in the further growth and in the
evolution of new trees."

"There is one eternal thinker," said Subhûti, "thinking non-eternal thoughts, and
the eternal thinker is the Self."

"Would not your statement be truer,"
interrupted Anuruddha, "if reversed: there
are eternal thoughts which are thought by
non-eternal thinkers? In other words, what we
call a thinker is but the thinking of the thought;
and the thinking of true thoughts is the attainment of the eternal. The Truth is the Immortal, the truth is Nirvâna."

There was a lull in the conversation and
after a pause the Buddhist monk continued:

"Your Katha-Upanishad is a discourse on the problem; it is a formulation of the How as to the hereafter, but instead of giving an answer, it merely builds up a beautiful air-castle. The true solution is only given in the doctrine of the Tathâgata."

The Brahman chief felt that his most sacred convictions were omitted in this statement, and he asked, not without a tremor of uneasiness in his voice: "Is there nothing in me that is immutable, nothing that is eternal and immortal?"

"Whether or not there is anything immortal in you," was Anuruddha's reply, "depends solely upon yourself. If you consist of thoughts that are pure and holy, you are pure and holy; if you consist of thoughts that are sinful, you are sinful; and if you consist of immortal truth, you are immortal. The attainment of truth is immortality, and to do the work of truth is Nirvâna."

Subhûti shook his head. "I want to possess the truth, but I do not want to lose my own identity."

"And I," enjoined Anuruddha, "want the

truth to possess me so as to lose myself in the cause of the Truth. What a blessing it is to have a higher purpose in life than self!"

Subhûti gazed at his friend in amazement: "What shall I be after the dissolution of my body in death? I shrink from losing my Self. Should there be nothing that I can call my own?"

"Let my reply," rejoined Anuruddha, "be in the words of the Blessed One, who said:

> "'Naught follows him who leaves this life;
> For all things must be left behind:
> Wife, daughters, sons, one's kin, and friends,
> Gold, grain, and wealth of every kind.
> But every deed a man performs,
> With body, or with voice, or mind,
> 'Tis this that he can call his own,
> This will he never leave behind.

> "'Deeds, like a shadow, ne'er depart:
> Bad deeds can never be concealed;
> Good deeds cannot be lost and will
> In all their glory be revealed.
> Let all, then, noble deeds perform,
> As seeds sown in life's fertile field;
> For merit gained this life within,
> Rich blessings in the next will yield.'"

Having quoted the words of the Blessed One, Anuruddha continued: "Your deeds are your own and will remain your own forever and aye. Your thoughts, your words, your actions are not gone when they are past; they stay with you. They are the living stones of which the structure of your being is built up. And there is no power in heaven nor upon earth, nor even in hell, by which you can get rid of them. Your life-history is your Self, your actual self, and as your life-history continues after your death, so your identical self will remain. When we pass away we shall continue to live according to our deeds."

THE EPIDEMIC

THREE children were born to the young couple, and all three were boys full of promise. Sudatta's prospects were brighter than he had ever dared to hope. But times change and misfortunes overcome men sometimes when least expected. A drought set in, which dried up all the wells of the country, spreading famine and contagious disease. The people prayed to the gods, they fasted and expiated their sins, the priests offered sacrifices and recited incantations, but the rain did not fall. More sacrifices were offered, and the blood of slaughtered animals reeked to heaven; yet the drought continued; the gods remained deaf to the prayers of the priests; the famine became worse, and the disease caused more ravage than before.

Subhûti, the chief, did all he could to alleviate the sorry lot of his afflicted people. He was a rich man, but his wealth proved insufficient to feed the poor.

Sudatta did his best in ministering unto the sick. Having learned from his father, the village priest whose office it was to gather the sacred herbs for sacrifices, the virtues of various plants, he brewed medicinal drinks for assuaging the sufferings of the patients and he was aided in his work by Subhûti his noble father-in-law and Kacchâyana,
his brother-in-law.

When at last the epi-

demic began to abate, it came to pass that Subhûti the chief himself fell sick. At first it seemed that he was merely exhausted through

night-watches and grief, but soon it became
apparent that he was affected by the disease

and his condition grew very critical. His relatives gathered at his bedside and were inconsolable.

He had been so faithful in his kindness to every one that they thought they could not live without him; but he himself remained serene and self-possessed. Having blessed his sons, his daughter, and grand-children, he comforted them, saying: "Cease sorrowing; there is no loss in this body of flesh; it is outworn by old age and disease like a garment. If you cherish with faithful hearts the example that I set you, death can never separate us."

When the evening came, Subhûti sent away his daughter and grand-children, keeping only Kacchâyana and Sudatta with him. And when the pain of the disease for a while abated, he said: "The sufferings which I witnessed opened mine eyes and I have understood the four noble truths proclaimed by the Tathâgata. I feel that my life is ebbing away, but I am not troubled in my mind, for death has lost its terrors. Wherever I shall be reborn, I am confident that it will be on a higher plane and I shall be a step nearer the holy goal Nirvâna.''

"Surely, father," rejoined Sudatta, "after a long life spent in doing good, thou deservest a high reward, which will be nothing less than the bliss of Brahma's heaven.''

Rallying all his strength once more, Subhûti replied: "Speak not of rewards while there are duties to be performed. Brahma's heaven is made for those who cling to the thought of Self. I am confident that this present incarnation of mine shall have peace; but not my love for mankind; not my sympathy with those who suffer; not my truth-seeking mind. So long as there is suffering in the world I shall never entertain any desire to ascend into a heaven of bliss; I want to be reborn in the depths of hell. There the misery is greatest and salvation most needed. That is the best place to enlighten those in darkness, to rescue what is lost, and to point out the path to those who have gone astray.''

With these words Subhûti fell back exhausted. He murmured with a broken voice the refuge formula of the Buddhists, saying:

"I take my refuge in the Buddha,
I take my refuge in the Dharma,
I take my refuge in the Sangha."

Having thus given expression to the faith that was in him, his eyes, which had just before been sparkling with noble enthusiasm, grew dim, and he passed away peacefully.

A holy stillness pervaded the room.

*
*   *

And it happened that very evening that Anuruddha passed through Kuduraghara and when he came to the mansion of Subûhti he found his friend the chief no longer among the living. He saluted Kacchâyana and Sudatta and sat down with them in silence.

The sun sank down and Kacchâyana lit a candle, but no one spoke a word.

When the night advanced Anuruddha raised his sonorous voice and sang:

> "How transient are things mortal!
> How restless is man's life!
> But Peace stands at the portal
> Of Death, and ends all strife.

> "Life is a constant parting—
> One more the stream has crossed;
> But think ye who stand smarting
> Of that which ne'er is lost.

"All rivers flowing, flowing,
    Must reach the distant main ;
The seeds which we are sewing
    Will ripen into grain."

COPYING THE MANUSCRIPT

KACCHÂYANA joined Anuruddha on his journey to Râjagaha, and when he saw the Blessed One and heard him explain the doctrine, he entered the order of samanas and became a man of repute among them on account of his wisdom. When he returned home he retired into the forest near Kuduraghara to a place called the Precipice, and the people of his village called him Mahâ-Kacchâyana, for although they, being Brahmans, looked upon him as a heretic, they respected him and said: "He is one of the great disciples of the Blessed One, well versed in both, the Brahman and Buddhist Scriptures, and we know that he has attained the highest degree of scholarship and sanctity."

Sudatta had lost his faith in the religion of his fathers, without, however, adopting the new faith of the Buddhists. One day, when walk-

ing with his brother-in-law through the village,
he said: "Is it not sad to lose a father or any
one whom we dearly love? Truly there is no
doctrine that can take away the pangs of grief
and afford genuine comfort."

"My dear brother," replied Kacchâyana,
"so long as your aim is to escape suffering
for your own person, you are not yet free. Let
the pain of your grief have its way, and do not
try to be exempt from the natural law to
which all mortals are subject alike."

"But consider," objected the other one,
"the terrible fate of the dead. Is it not an
awful thought that their whole existence is
wiped out as if they had never been?"

"There you are mistaken," suggested Kacchâyana. Death is a dissolution, but man's
existence is not wiped out as though he had
never been, for every deed of his continues in
its peculiar identity."

A sad smile appeared on Sudatta's face when
he interrupted his brother-in-law: "That is
nothing more than a mode of speech. If the
dead continue to live, please tell me where is
our father now?"

Kacchâyana replied: "Is he not here with us?" And after a pause he continued: "It is with men as with books. You can write vile things or good and noble thoughts upon palm leaves. The book does not consist of leaves but of ideas. The leaves are mere material for the scribe, and there are thousands of leaves on the palms that will never be turned into books. When our father, the venerable Subhûti, pondered over the problem of death, he composed the Katha-Upanishad which appeared to me more valuable than any one I had ever heard or read. He wrote it upon the leaves of the big palm-tree in our garden. When the leaves were bleached and prepared for writing, our venerable father scratched the words of the Upanishad into the leaves, and when he died left them to me as my most precious inheritance, for they are not treasures of worldly goods, but a monument of his meditations which contains his immortal soul. Formerly I held them dear because I valued them as a specimen of his hand-writing, but now I deem his thoughts to be of higher worth. During the great drought the leaves became worm-eaten, and they are now breaking to pieces. I have the whole Upanishad in my memory, but knowing that when I die the thoughts expressed in the book will be lost, I have begun to transcribe them, line by line, carefully, from the rotten leaves of the old manuscript. I shall lend the new copy to other scribes, and the Katha-Upanishad will be preserved and become known in other lands and to other generations. The old copy has become illegible and has partly crumbled into dust, but the thoughts will not die, for they are re-embodied in the new copy. It is in this same way that we, our aspirations, our ideas, our mind, will be preserved. The character of the present generation is impressed upon the coming generation by our acts, our words, and our sentiments, and when we die we pass away but continue according to our deeds. All that is compounded must be dissolved again; the palm-leaves wither, but the Katha-Upanishad still lives."

"Would it not be glorious," exclaimed Sudatta, "if both could be preserved—the copy of the book and the thought contained in it?"

" I would hesitate to echo your sentiment,"
rejoined Kacchâyana : " Do you remember the
beautiful words of Anuruddha which found an
echo in that same Upanishad? He said : ' Choose
not the dearer, choose the truer, for the truer
is the better.' At that time I chose the dearer,
but life has taught me a lesson ; I have now
chosen the truer, and the truer has become the
dearer to me."

" Has it, indeed? " queried Sudatta, without
concealing his surprise.

" Indeed it has," was Kacchâyana's reply.
" Death is not only necessary in life, as the
inevitable corollary of birth, but it is also a
most salutary arrangement. There is no more
reason to speak of the horrors of death than to
speak of the horrors of sleep. Indeed there is
a beauty in death ; and it is the beauty of
death that lends consecration to life. Think
only of what life would be without death ; a
monotonous and thoughtless sporting in pleasures and nothing more. It is death that makes
time precious. Death sets us to thinking and
makes religion necessary. Death alone forces
us to give value to life. If there were no death,

there would be no heroes, no sages, no Buddhas.   Therefore, death is inevitable; yet it
is not an evil.   Fools shudder at the mere
thought of it; but the wise fear it not.   For
death is our teacher, and also our benefactor."

YOUNG SUBHÛTI

SUDATTA'S boys grew up and took charge of the land that they had inherited from their grandfather. Their assistance made it possible for Sudatta to gain more leisure for himself, and he began frequently to retire to the Precipice, in the loneliness of the forest, where Kacchâyana lived, and devoted himself to study and meditation. Although only in the forties, his hair had turned white and he might easily have passed for an older man, who, however, in his old age, preserved unusual vigor and health. The people of the village called him whenever there was sickness in the family, and he was always willing to help them in their troubles with counsel and personal assistance.

In those days it came to pass that Bimbisâra, the king, died, and his son Ajâtasattu ascended the throne.

Ajâtasattu sent envoys to all the cities and
villages of his kingdom and also to all the
neighboring countries that were subject to his
sceptre, to test the allegiance of his people.
And the King's envoy, surrounded by a staff
of counsellors and accompanied by a military

escort, came also to Kuduraghara. When
they entered Kuduraghara they were told, on

inquiring for the chief of the village, that
since the death of Mahâ-Subhûti the people
had been liv-
ing without a
chief. Then the
King's envoy

had the people assembled, and requested them
to choose a new magistrate whom the King,

Ajâtasattu, should install in the place of
Mahâ-Subhûti. Seeing that Kacchâyana had
retired from the world to live a religious life,
and that Sudatta appeared to be quite advanced in years, he presented as a candidate
Sudatta's oldest son who was called Subhûti
after his grandfather; and when the people
saw him in his manliness they hailed him
and shouted, "Let young Subhûti be our
chief; let the King appoint him successor to
Mahâ-Subhûti."

Some of the older men in the assembly were
greatly pleased with the new chief and said:
"If Mahâ-Subhûti were to reappear bodily
among us in the vigor of his youth, he could
not look different from this noble youth.
Mahâ-Subhûti was exactly like him when
King Bimbisâra installed him in office."

THE BLESSED ONE

ONE day a stranger passed through Kuduraghara, and, meeting Sudatta in the street, asked him the road to Râjagaha. The old Brahman pointed out the way to the capital of the country, and said: "I should like to go to Râjagaha myself, for there the Blessed One lives, the Holy Buddha, who is the teacher of gods and men. He is the master whose doctrine I profess."

"Why not join me?" said the stranger. "I am Chandra, the gambler. Having heard of the wisdom of the Blessed Buddha, I made up my mind to go to Râjagaha and reap the benefits of his instruction."

Sudatta took leave of his friends and joined Chandra, the gambler, on his way to Râjagaha, and, remembering a wish once uttered by his father-in-law, he took with him the palm-leaf manuscript of the Katha-Upanishad.

While they were travelling together on the highroad, Chandra said: "Deep is the wis-

dom of the Perfect One.   He teaches that existence is suffering, and my experience confirms the doctrine. Pessimism is indeed the true theory of life."

"What do you mean by Pessimism?" interrupted Sudatta.

"Pessimism means that the world is bad," replied Chandra; and he continued: "The world is like a lottery in which there are few prizes and innumerable blanks. We can see at once how true it is that life is not worth living by supposing a wealthy man buying all the chances in a lottery in order to make sure of winning all the prizes. He would certainly be a loser. Life is bankrupt throughout; it is like a business enterprise which does not pay its expenses."

"My friend," said the Brahman, "I perceive that you are a man of experience. Am I right in assuming that, being a gambler, you had for a time an easy life until you met another gambler better versed in trickery than yourself, who cheated you out of all your possessions?"

"Indeed, sir," said the gambler, "that is my case exactly; and now I travel to the Blessed One, who has recognised the great truth that life is like a lost game in which the prizes are only baits for the giddy. Whenever I met a man unacquainted with gambling I always let him win in the beginning to make him bold. I, too, was for a time successful in the game of life, but now I know that those who win at first are going to lose more in the end than those who are frightened away by losing their first stake. Life uses the same tricks we use. I have been caught in the snare which I thought I had invented.''

Turning to the Brahman, bent with age and care, he continued: ''The whiteness of your beard and the wrinkles in your face indicate that you, too, have found the sweets of life bitter. I suppose you are not less pessimistic than myself.''

A beam of sunshine appeared in the Brahman's eyes and his gait became erect like that of a king. ''No, sir,'' he replied, ''I have no experience like yours. I tasted the sweets of life when I was young, many, many years ago. I have sported in the fields with my playmates. I have loved and was beloved, but I loved with a pure heart and there was

no bitterness in the sweets which I tasted.
My experience came when I saw the sufferings of life. The world is full of sorrow and
the end of life is death. I have been sad at
heart ever since, but when I think of the Buddha who has come into the world and teaches
us how to escape suffering I rejoice; I know
now that the bitterness of life is sweet to him
whose soul has found rest in Nirvâna."

"If life is full of bitterness, how can one
escape suffering?" asked Chandra.

And Sudatta replied: "We cannot escape
pain, but we can avoid evil, and it is by avoid-
ing evil we enter Nirvâna."

When the two men came to the Vihâra at
Râjagaha they approached the Blessed Buddha with clasped hands, saying: "Receive
us, O Lord, among thy disciples; permit us
to be hearers of thy doctrines; and let us take
refuge in the Buddha, the truth, and the community of Buddha's followers."

And the Holy One, who reads the secret
thoughts of men's minds, addressed Chandra,
the gambler, asking him: "Knowest thou, O
Chandra, the doctrine of the Blessed One?"

Chandra said: "I do. The Blessed One
teaches that life is misery."

And the Lord replied: "Life is misery indeed, but the Tathâgata hast come into the
world to point out the way
of salvation. His aim is to

teach men how to rescue themselves from misery. If thou art anxious for deliverance from

evil, enter the path with a resolute mind, sur-

render selfishness, practise self-discipline, and
work out thy salvation with diligence.''

"I came to the Blessed One to find peace,"
said the gambler, "not to undertake work."

Said the Blessed One: "Only by ener-
getic work can peace be found; death can be
conquered only by the resignation of self, and
only by strenuous effort is eternal bliss attained. Thou regardest the world as evil
because he who deceives will eventually be
ruined by his own devices. The happiness
that thou seekest is the pleasure of sin without sin's evil consequences. Men who have
not observed proper discipline, and have not
gained treasure in their youth, lie sighing for
the past. There is evil, indeed; but the evil
of which thou complainest is but the justice
of the law of karma. What a man has sown
that shall he reap."

Then the Blessed One turned to the Brahman, and, recognising the sterling worth of
his character, addressed him: "Verily, O
Brahman, thou understandest the doctrines of
the Tathâgata better than thy fellow-traveller.
He who makes the distress of others his own,
quickly understands the illusion of self. He
is like the lotus flower that grows in the wa-

ter, yet does the water not wet its petals. The pleasures of this world allure him not, and he will have no cause for regret.''

Searching with a friendly eye the benevolent features of his Brahman visitor, the Buddha continued: ''Thou art walking in the noble path of righteousness and thou delightest in the purity of thy work. If thou wishest to cure the diseases of the heart, as thou understandest how to heal the sores of the body, let people see the fruits that grow from the seeds of loving kindness. When they but know the bliss of a right mind they will soon enter the path and reach that state of steadiness and tranquillity in which they are above pleasure and pain, above the petty petulance of fretful desires, above sin and temptation. Go, then, back to thy home and announce to thy friends, who are subject to suffering, that he whose mind is free from the illusions of sinful desires will overcome the miseries of life. Spread goodness in words and deeds everywhere. In a spirit of universal kindness be ready to serve others with help and instruction; live happily, then, among the ailing;

among men who are greedy, remain free from greed; among men who hate, dwell free from hatred; and those who witness the blessings of a holy life will follow thee in the path of salvation."

Chandra listened with rapture to the words of the Blessed One and exclaimed: "Happy

is Sudatta! Oh! that I could understand the doctrine and practice it!"

The Blessed One said: "As the great ocean has only one taste, the taste of salt, so the doctrine of the Tathâgata has only one taste, the taste of salvation.

The eyes of the gambler were opened, and

his pessimism melted away in the sun of Buddha's doctrines. "O Lord," said he, "I long for that higher life to which the noble path of righteousness leads."

Said the Blessed One: "As sea-faring men are bent on reaching the haven of their destination, so all life presses forward to find the

bliss of enlightenment, and enlightenment alone can point out the way of righteousness that leads to Nirvâna."

The gambler folded his hands and said to the Buddha: "Wilt thou persuade the Brahman, my fellow-traveller, to take me to his home, where I am willing to enter his service that I may learn from him and attain to the same bliss?"

The Blessed One replied: "Let Sudatta the Brahman, do as he sees fit."

Sudatta, the Brahman, expressed his willingness to receive Chandra as a helpmate in his work, and added: "Anuruddha the philosopher taught me the path of the Dharma, which proclaims: 'Let evil deeds be covered by good deeds; he who was reckless and becomes sober, will brighten up the world like the moon when freed from clouds.'"

Seeing that the hearts of all present were ready to receive the good tidings of salvation, the Blessed One instructed them and roused and gladdened them with religious discourse, and having explained the doctrine, he concluded his sermon saying: "And this is the sign that you have reached the goal which is the glorious Nirvâna: No accident will ever be able to disturb your mind, for, in spite of the world's unrest, your heart will be like a still and smooth lake.   All attachment to Self has died out; it has become like a withered branch that no longer bears fruit.   But your sympathy goes out to every creature that suffers, and you are untiring in good works. Your heart beats higher; it expands and is roused to a nobler life; for it is inspired by the thoughts of the Buddha; your mind is clearer, for it now comprehends the length, the breadth, and the depth of existence, recognising the one goal that life must seek — Nirvâna.''